GRANNY'S SWEAR WORDS

COLORING BOOK FOR ADULTS

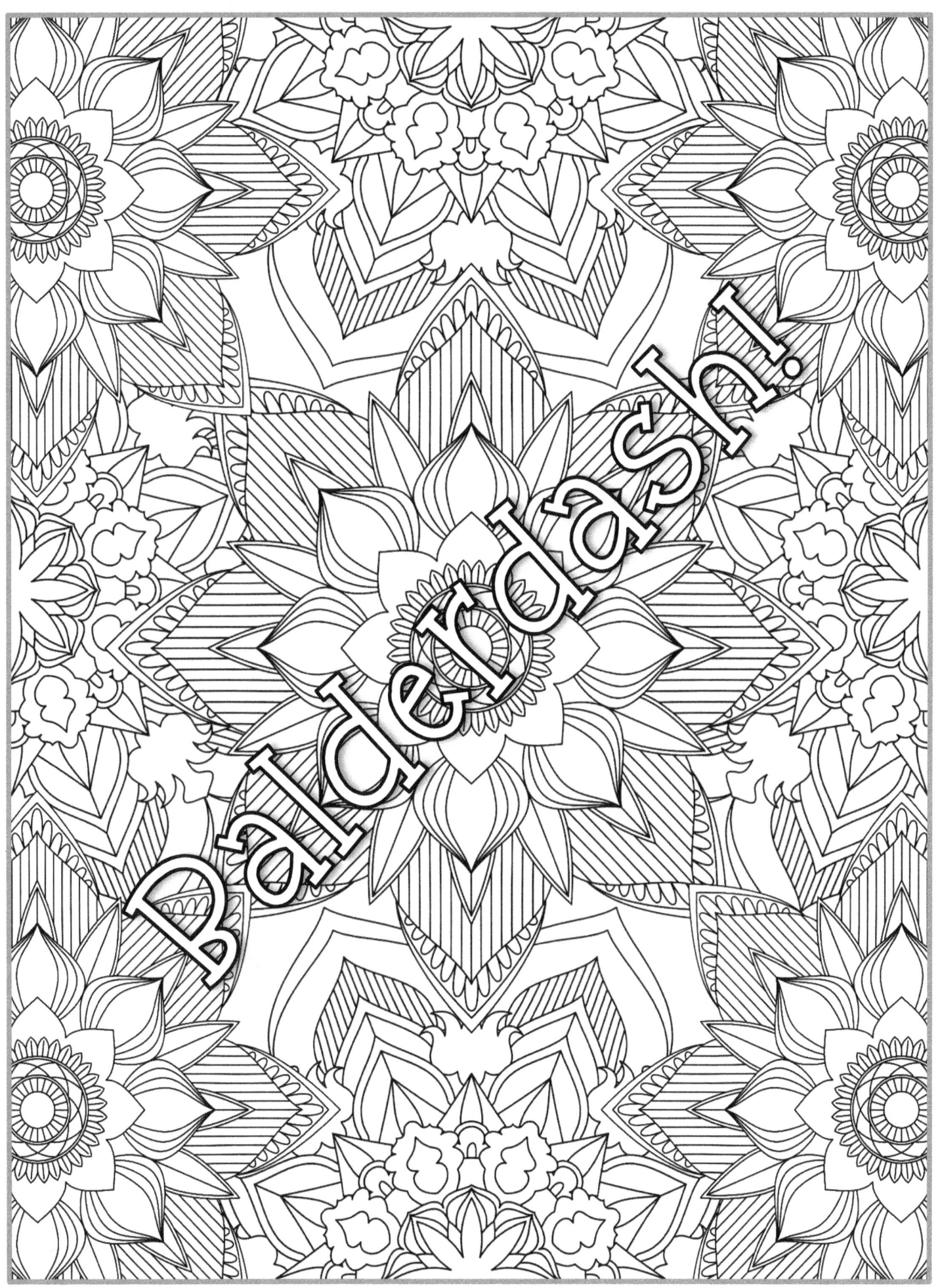

PAGE INTENTIONALLY LEFT BLANK FOR FRAMING.

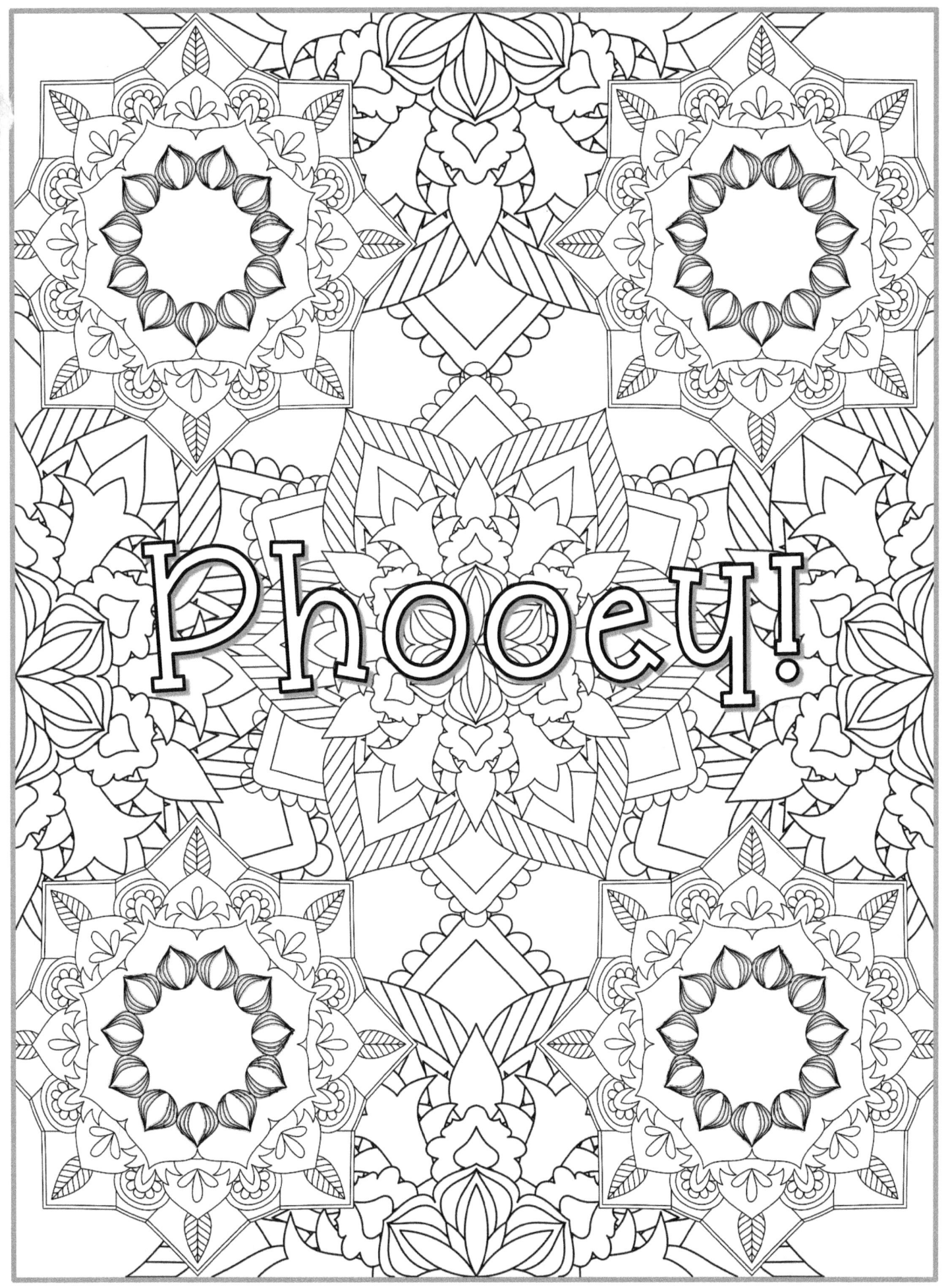

PAGE INTENTIONALLY LEFT BLANK FOR FRAMING.

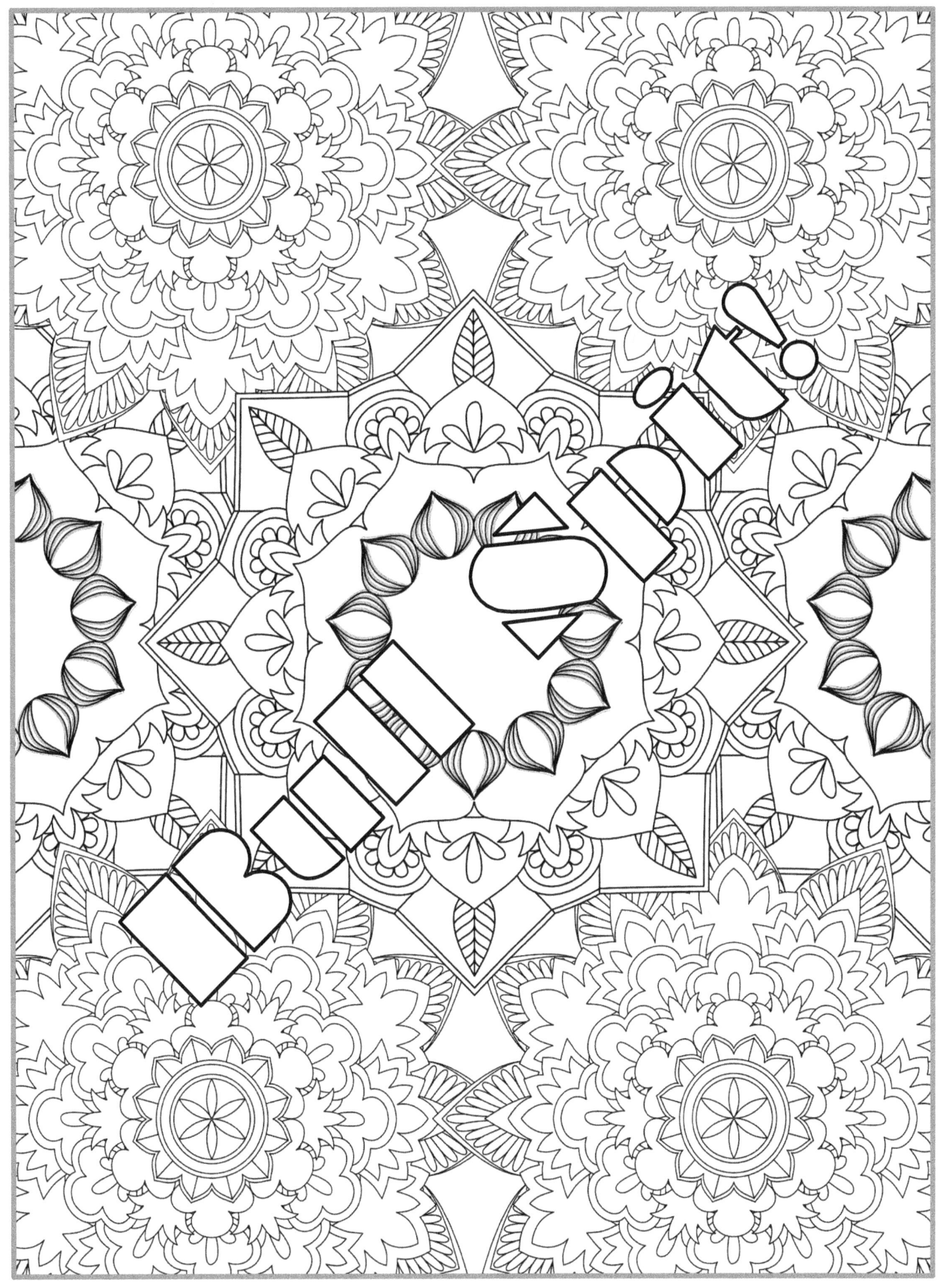

PAGE INTENTIONALLY LEFT BLANK FOR FRAMING.

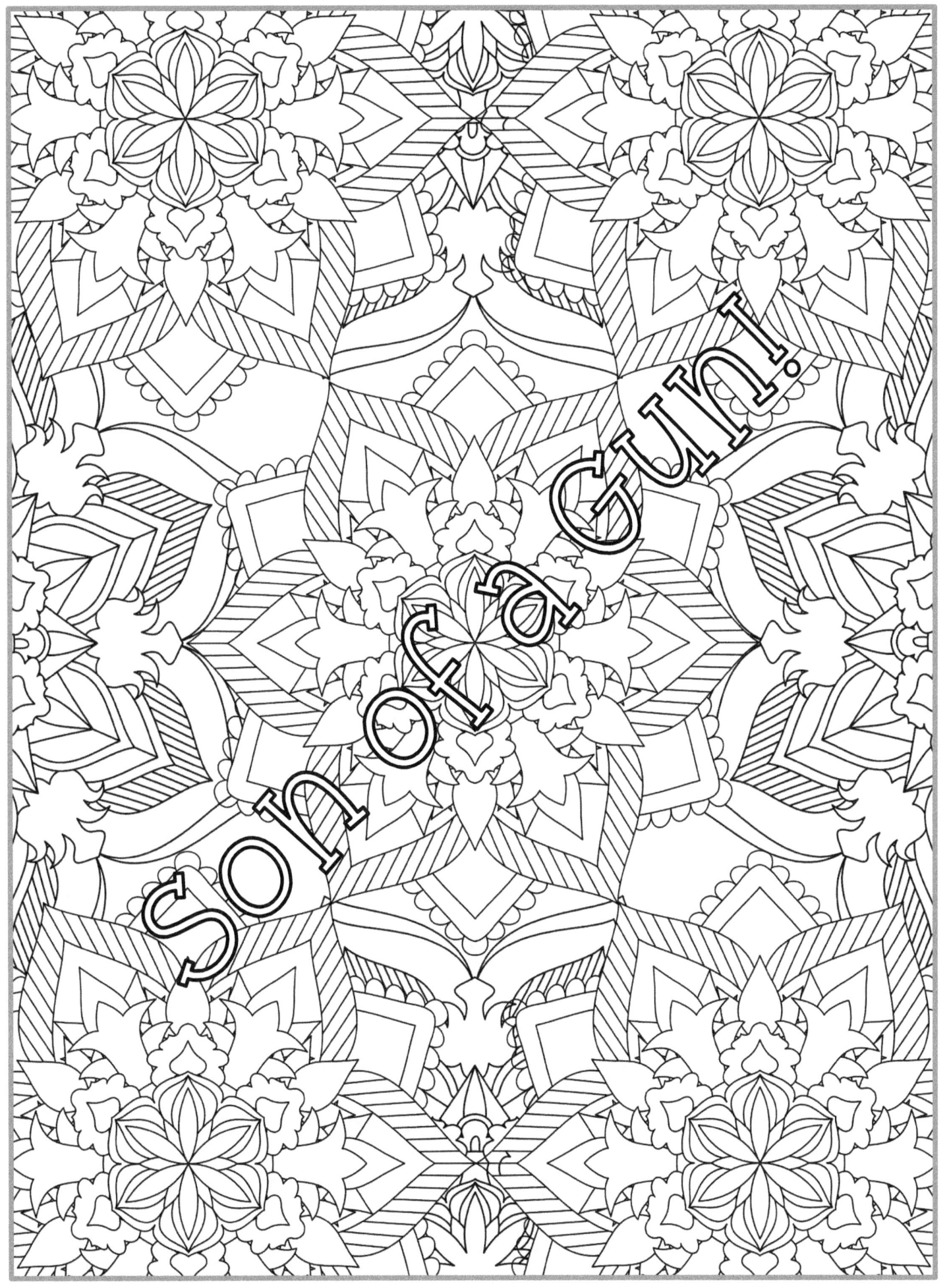

PAGE INTENTIONALLY LEFT BLANK FOR FRAMING.

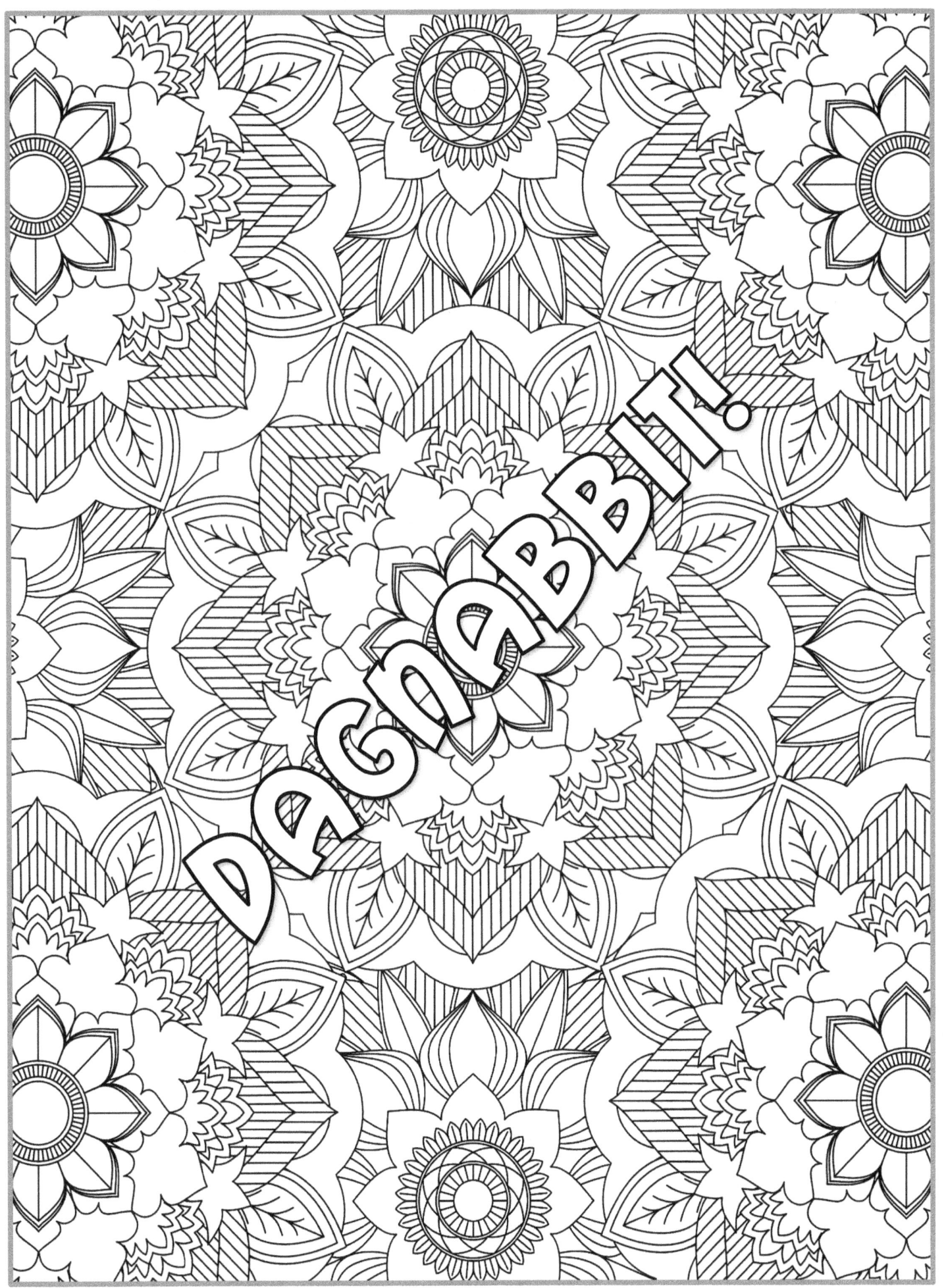

PAGE INTENTIONALLY LEFT BLANK FOR FRAMING.

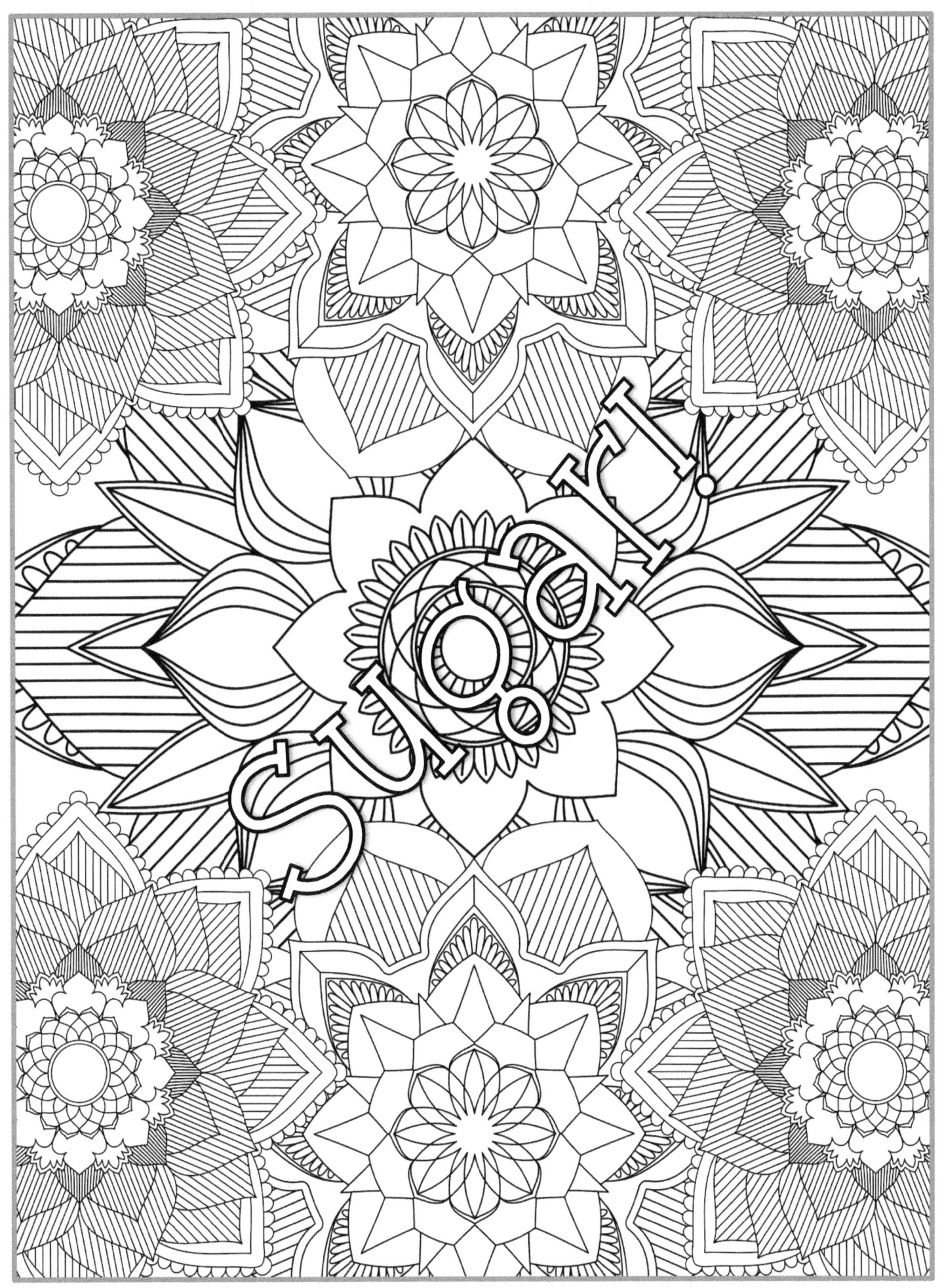

PAGE INTENTIONALLY LEFT BLANK FOR FRAMING.

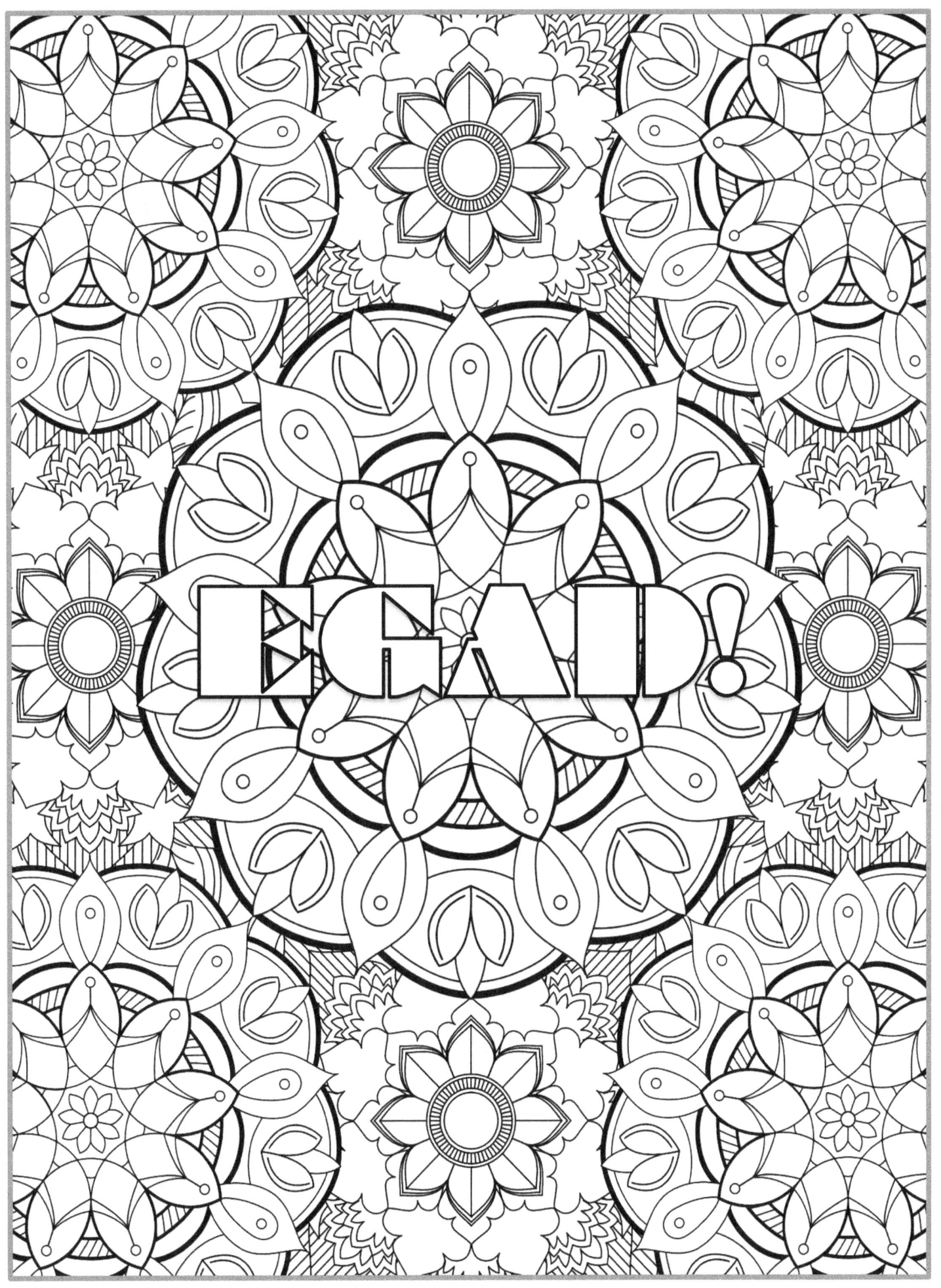

PAGE INTENTIONALLY LEFT BLANK FOR FRAMING.

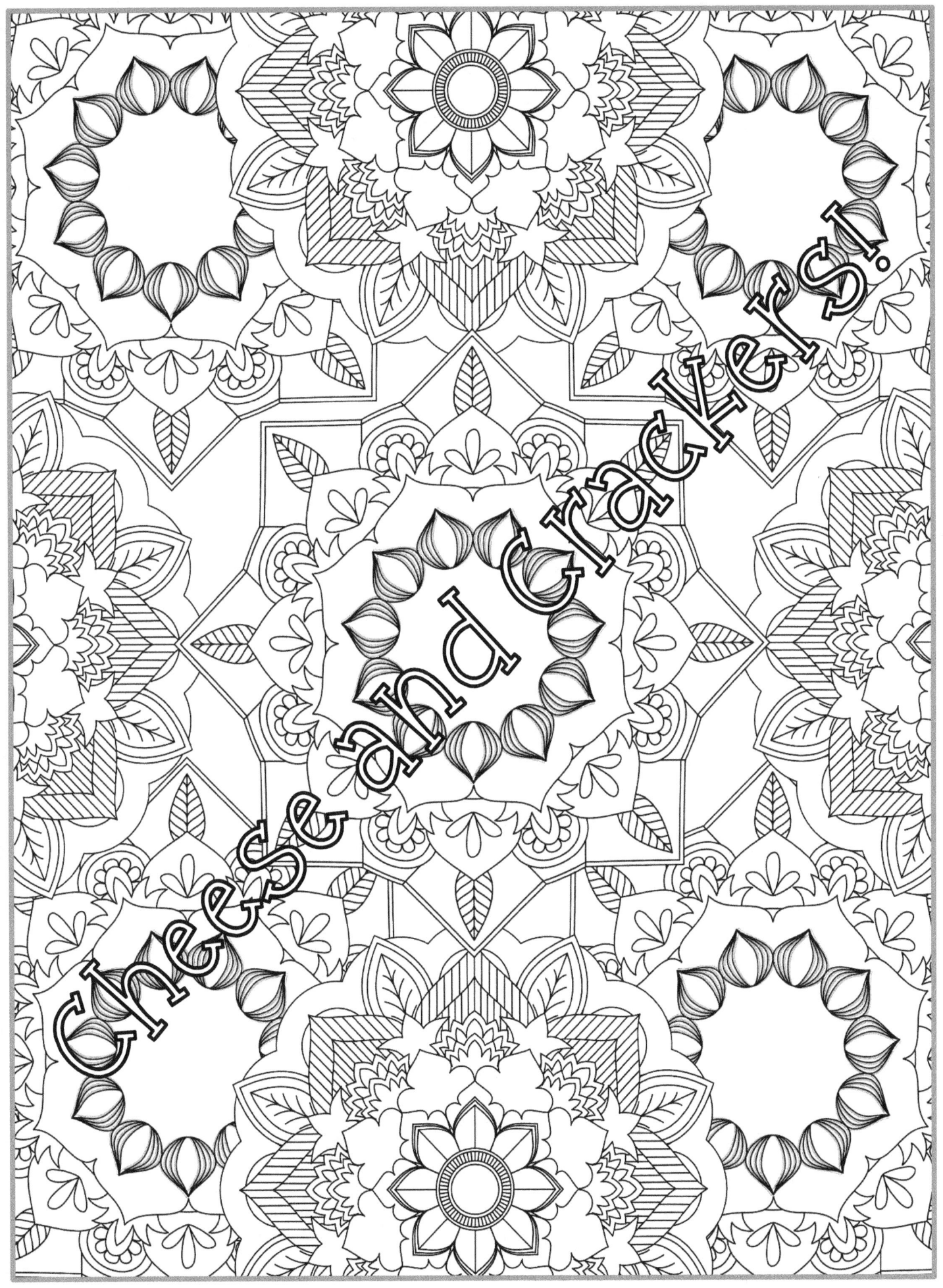

PAGE INTENTIONALLY LEFT BLANK FOR FRAMING.

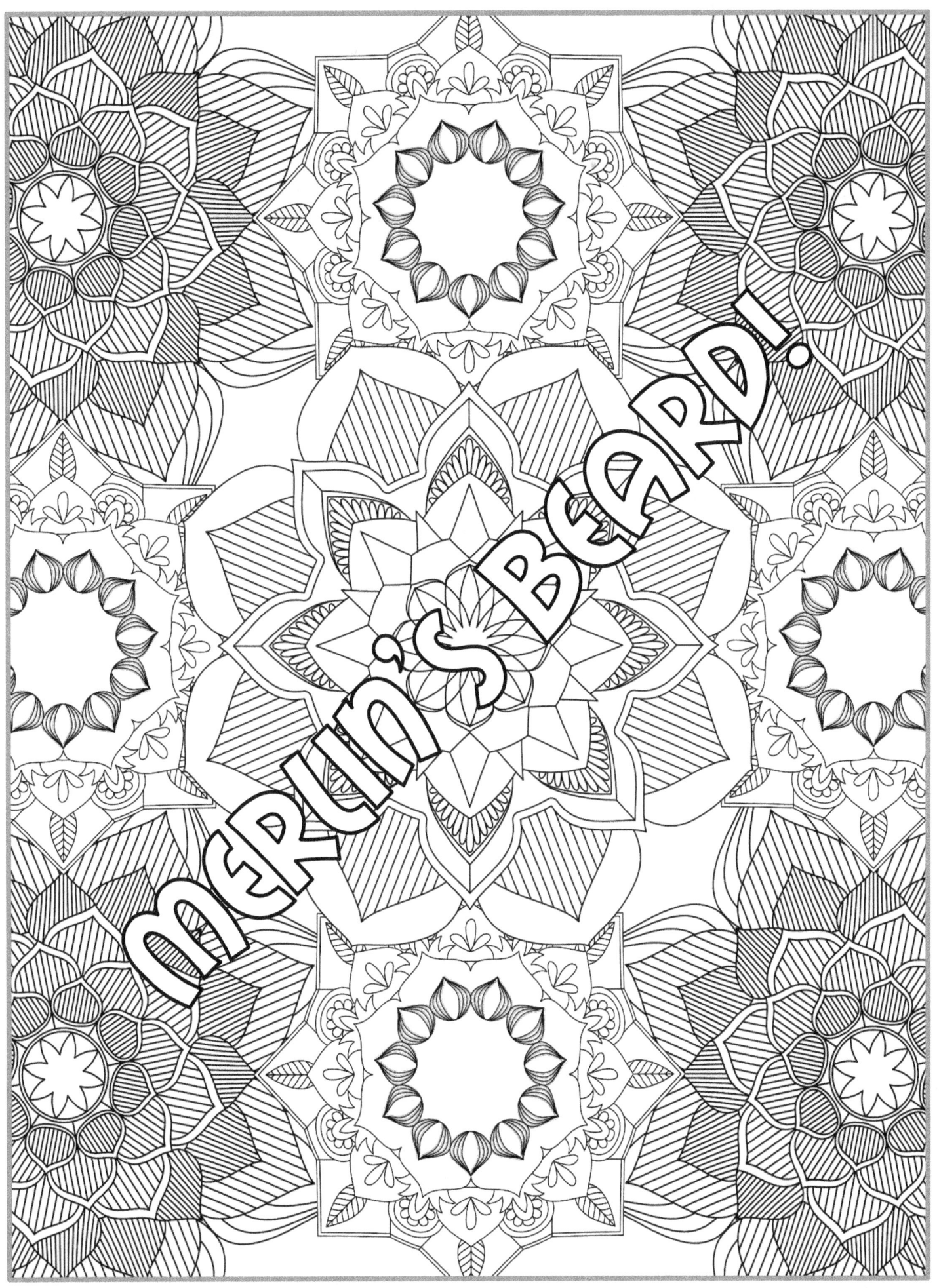

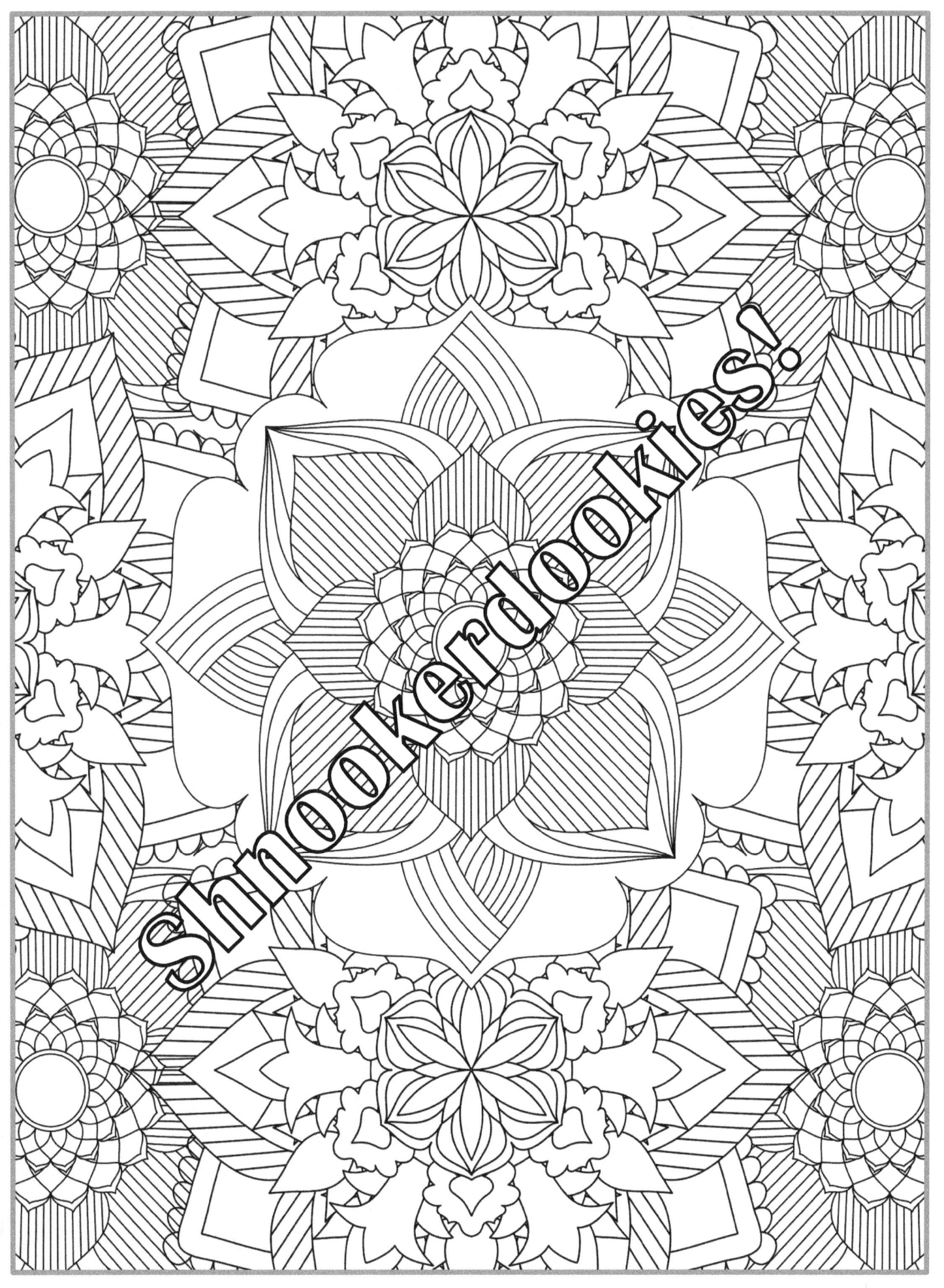

PAGE INTENTIONALLY LEFT BLANK FOR FRAMING.

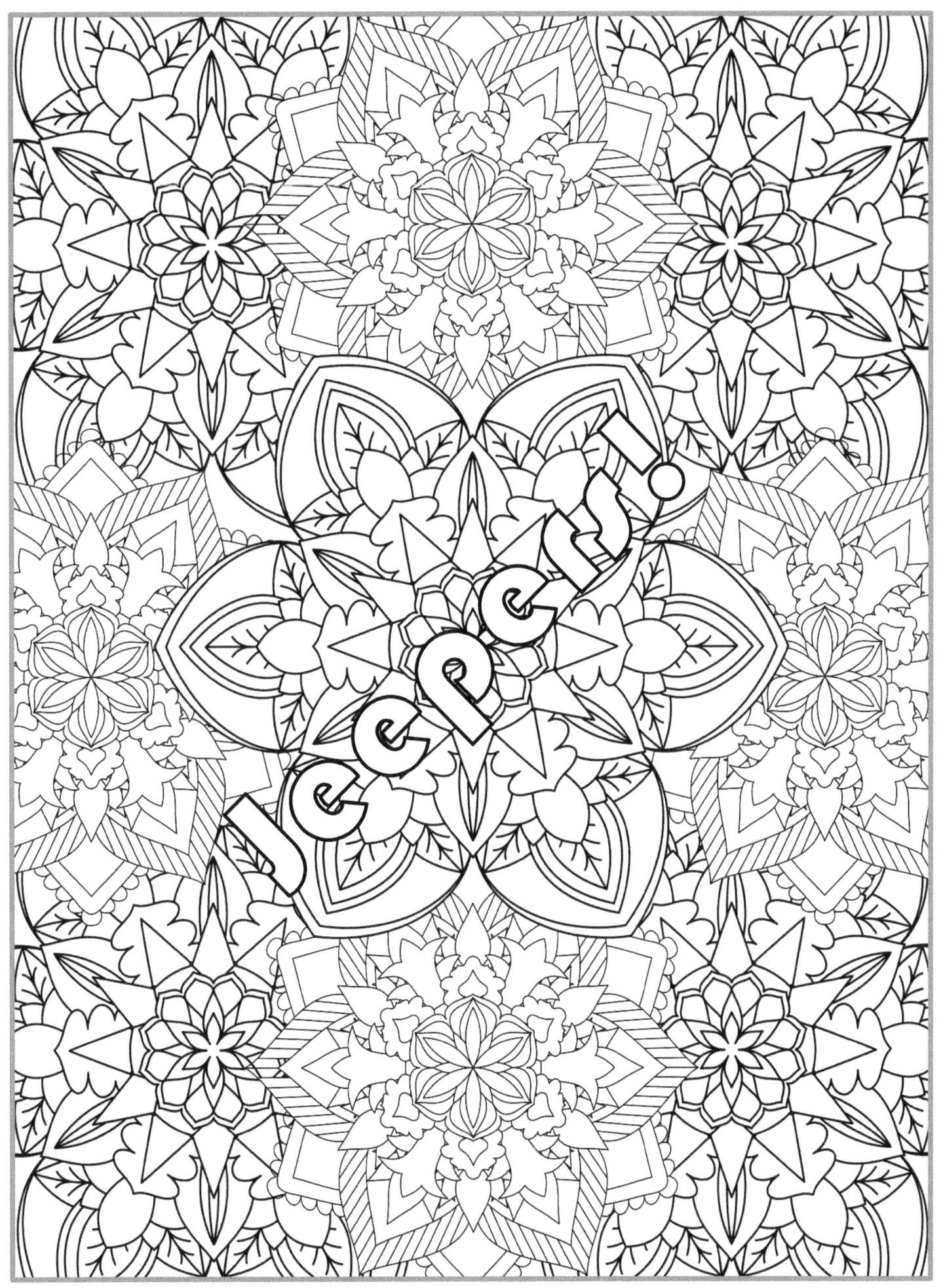

PAGE INTENTIONALLY LEFT BLANK FOR FRAMING.

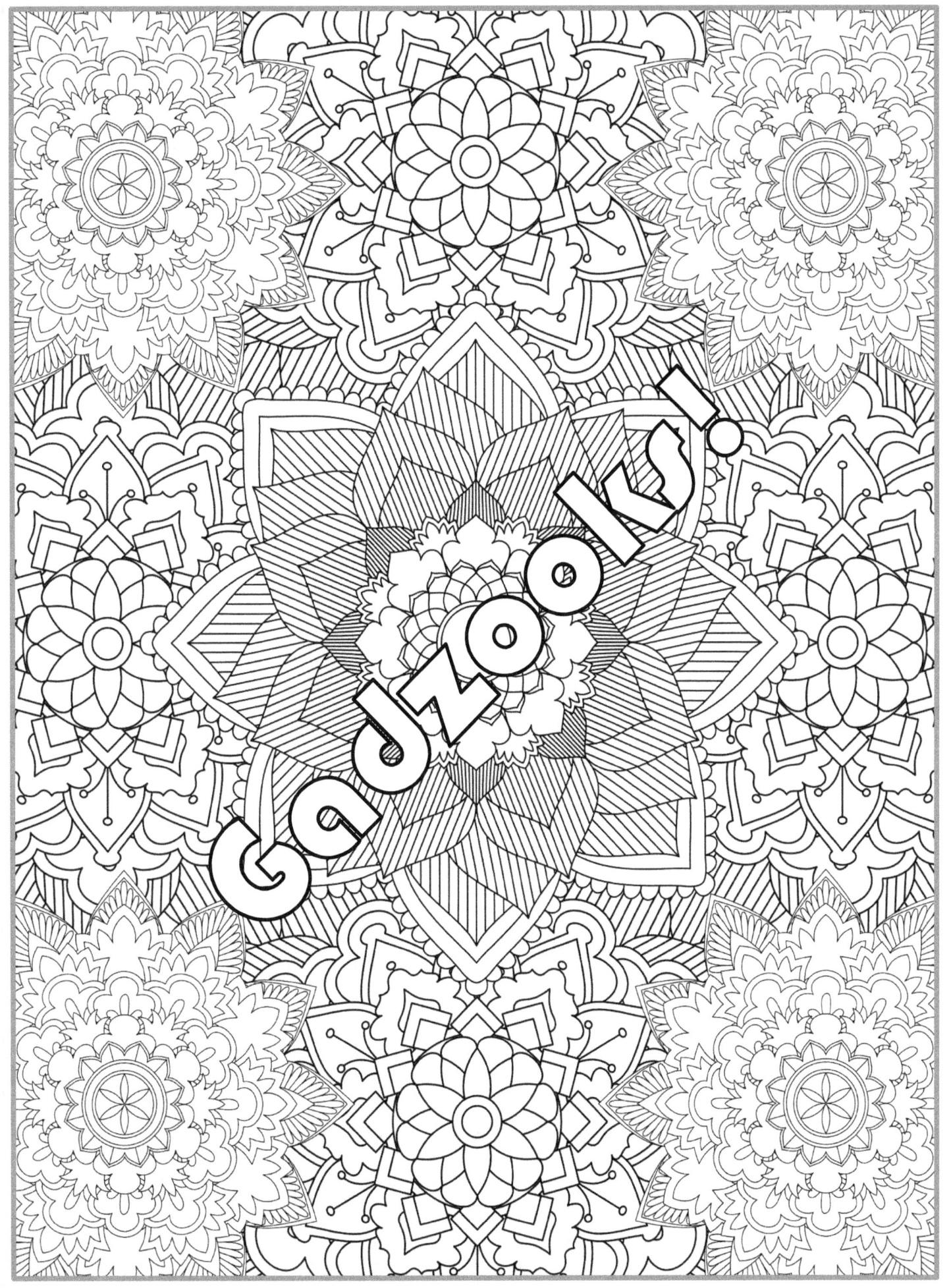

PAGE INTENTIONALLY LEFT BLANK FOR FRAMING.

PAGE INTENTIONALLY LEFT BLANK FOR FRAMING.

PAGE INTENTIONALLY LEFT BLANK FOR FRAMING.

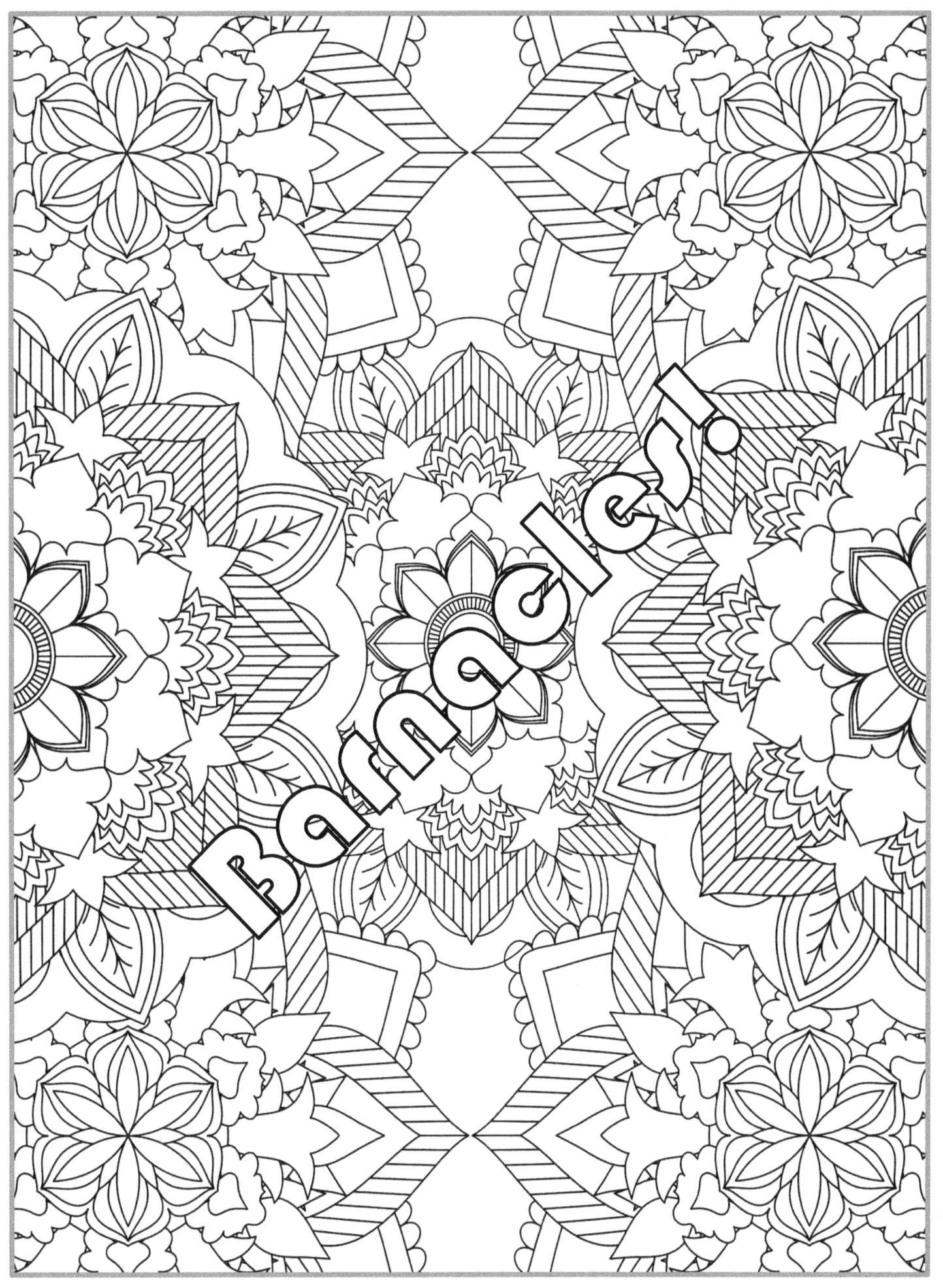

PAGE INTENTIONALLY LEFT BLANK FOR FRAMING.

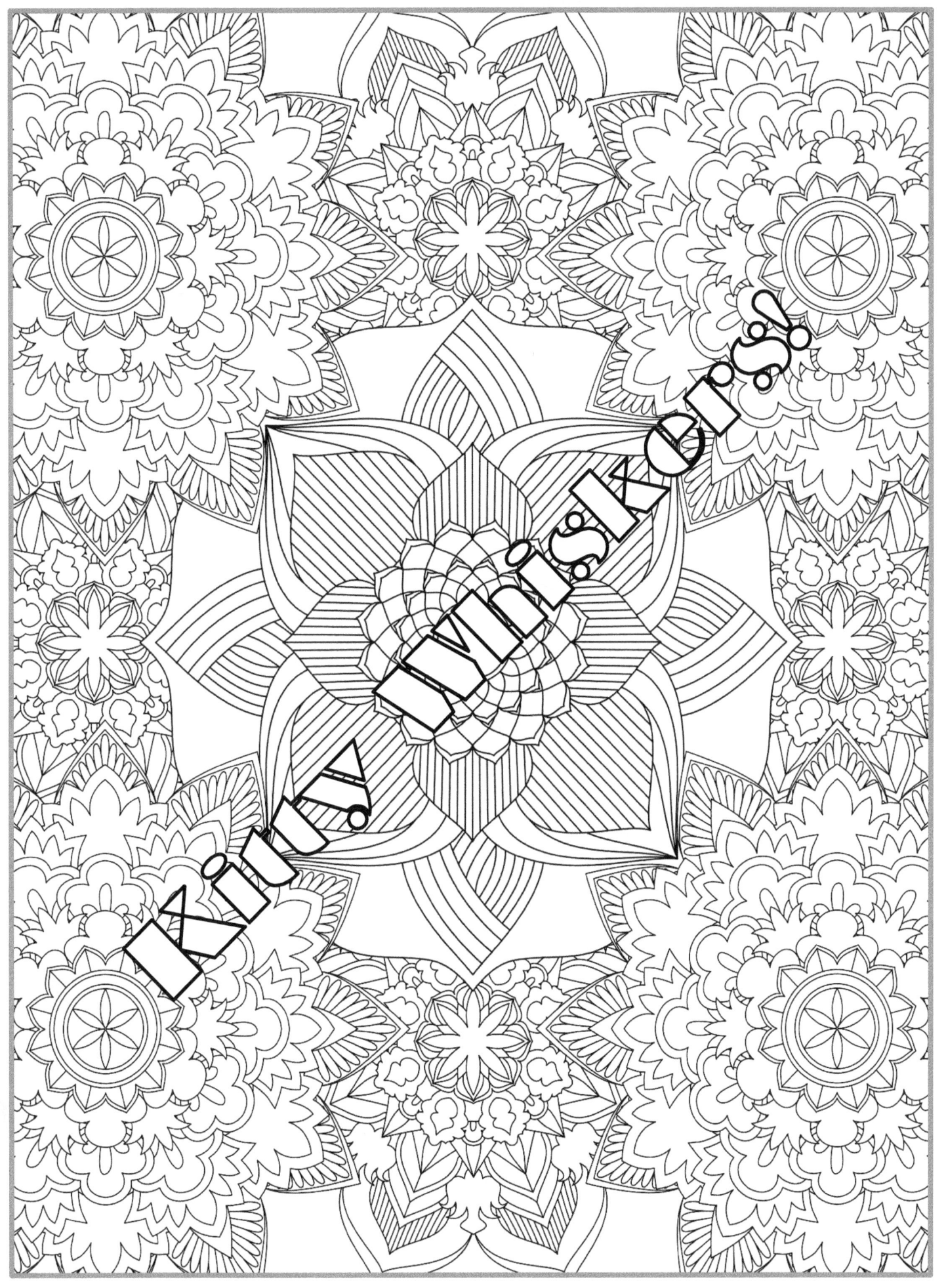

PAGE INTENTIONALLY LEFT BLANK FOR FRAMING.

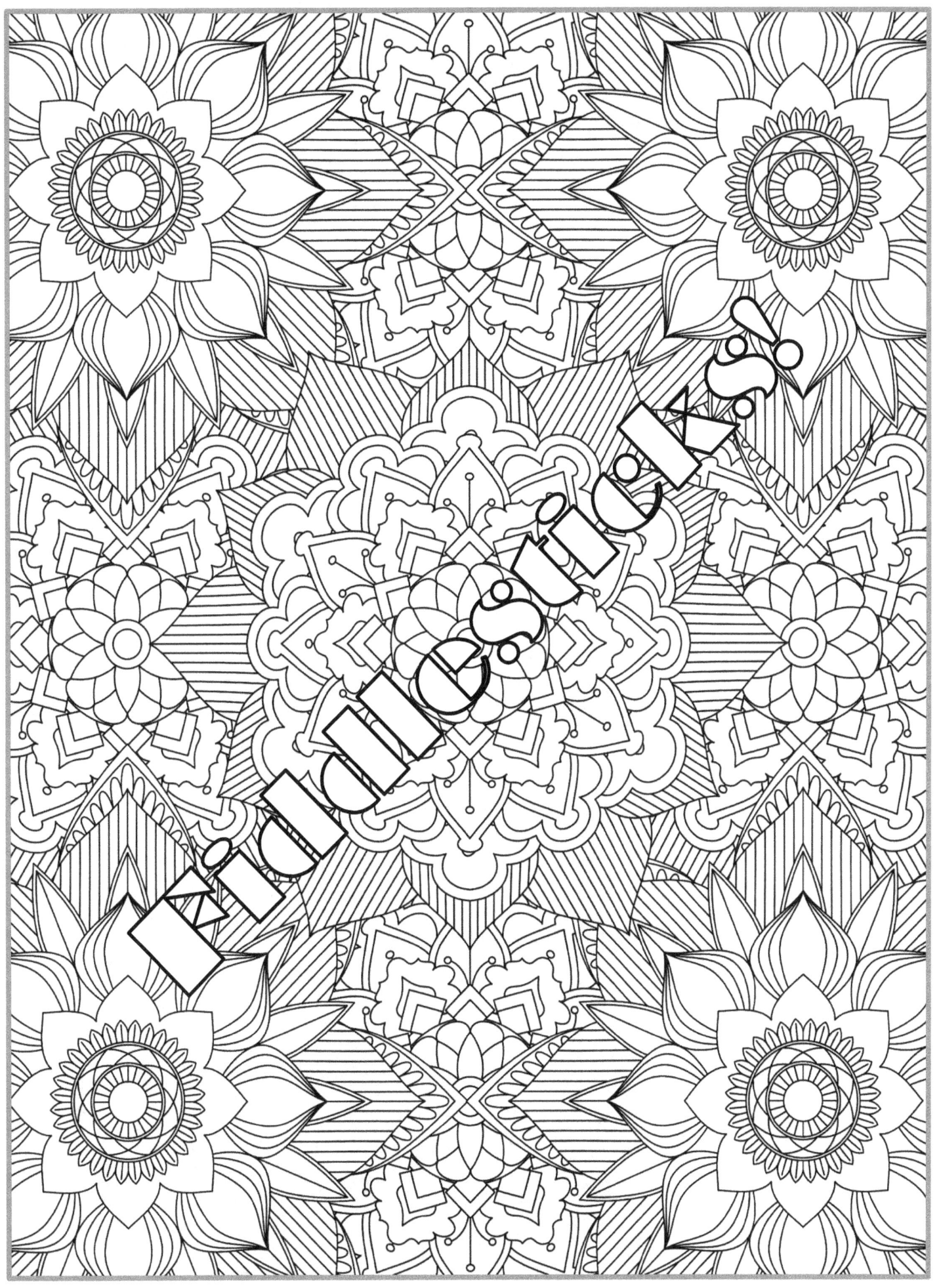

PAGE INTENTIONALLY LEFT BLANK FOR FRAMING.

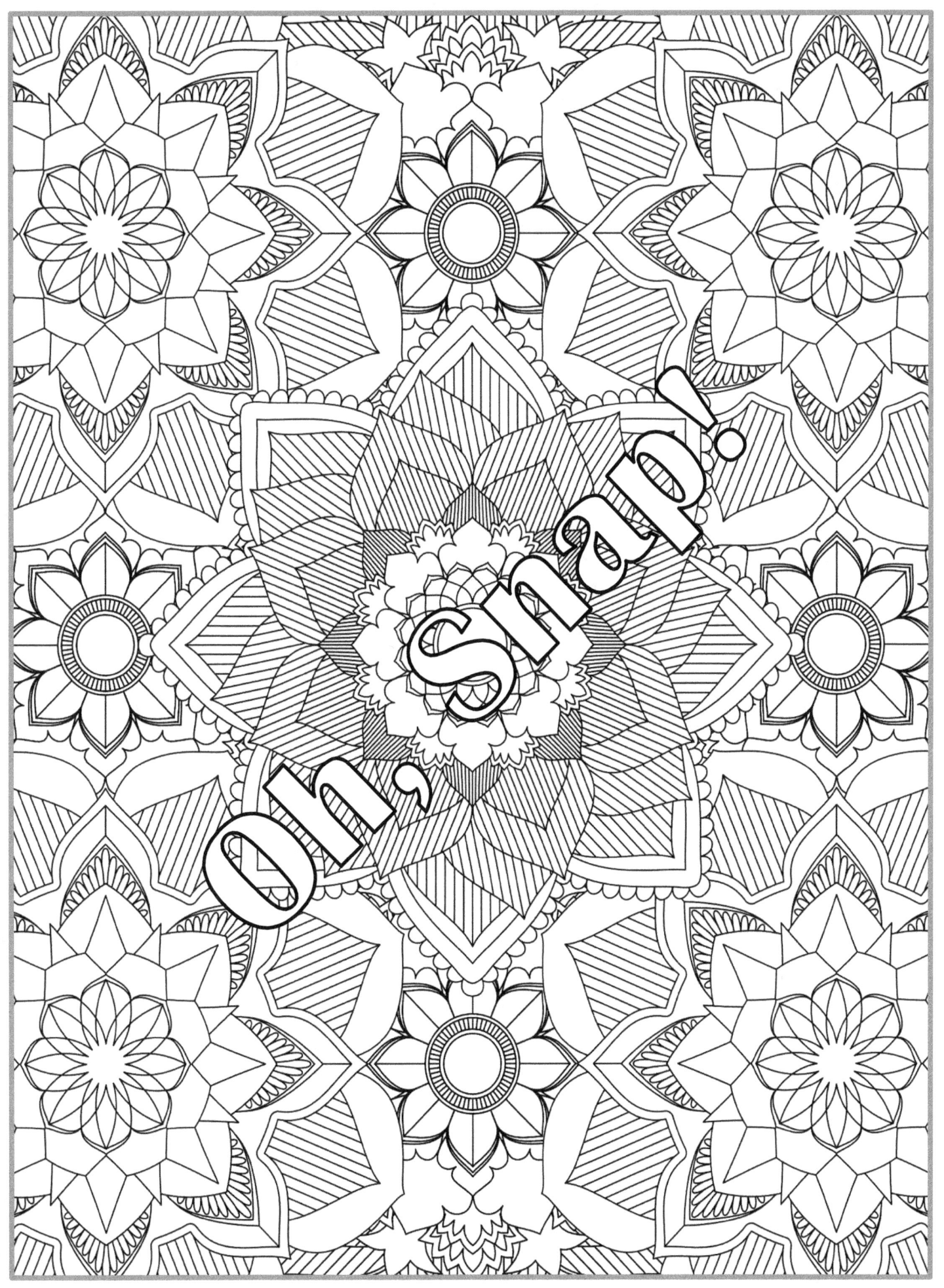

PAGE INTENTIONALLY LEFT BLANK FOR FRAMING.

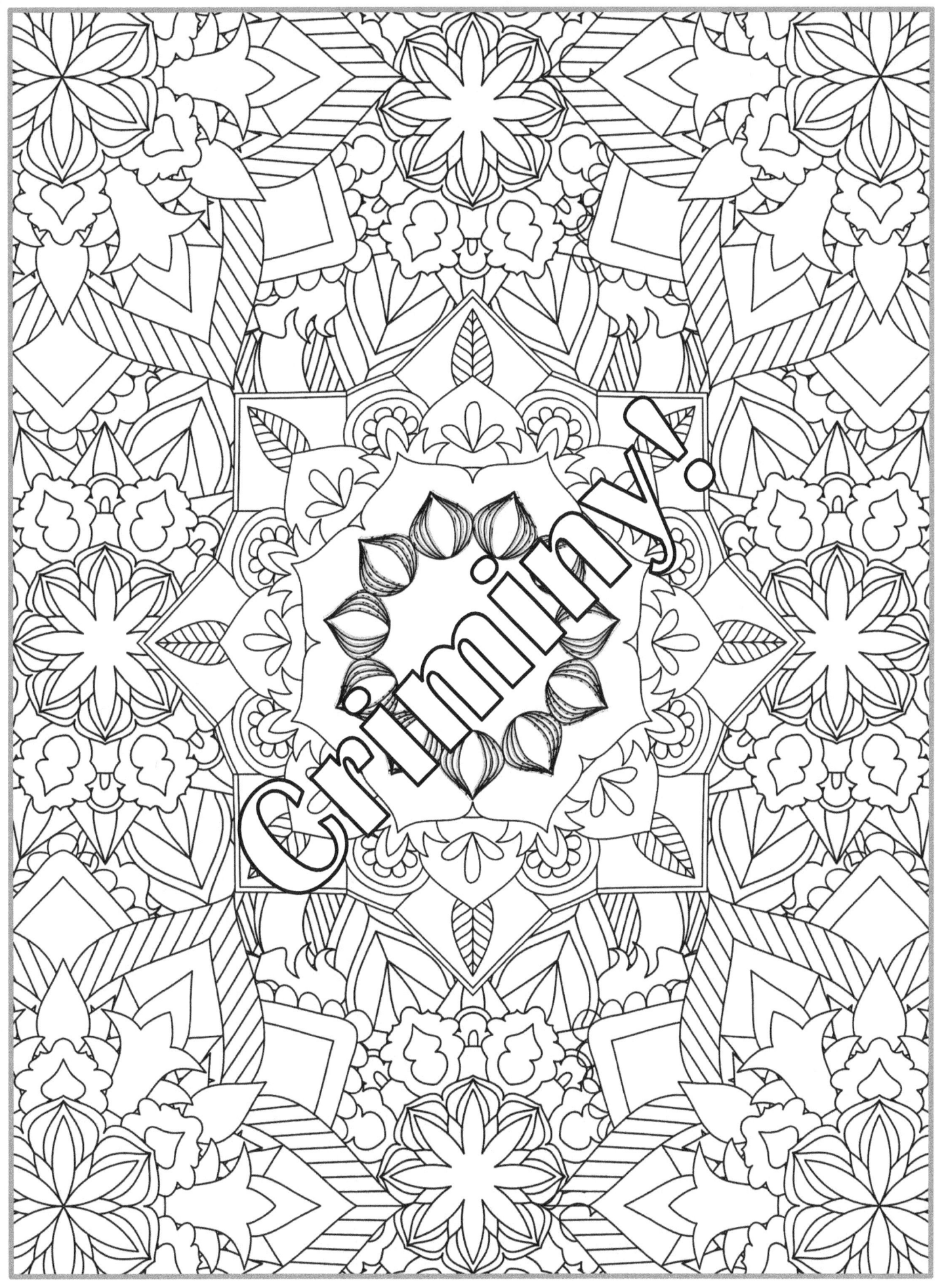

PAGE INTENTIONALLY LEFT BLANK FOR FRAMING.

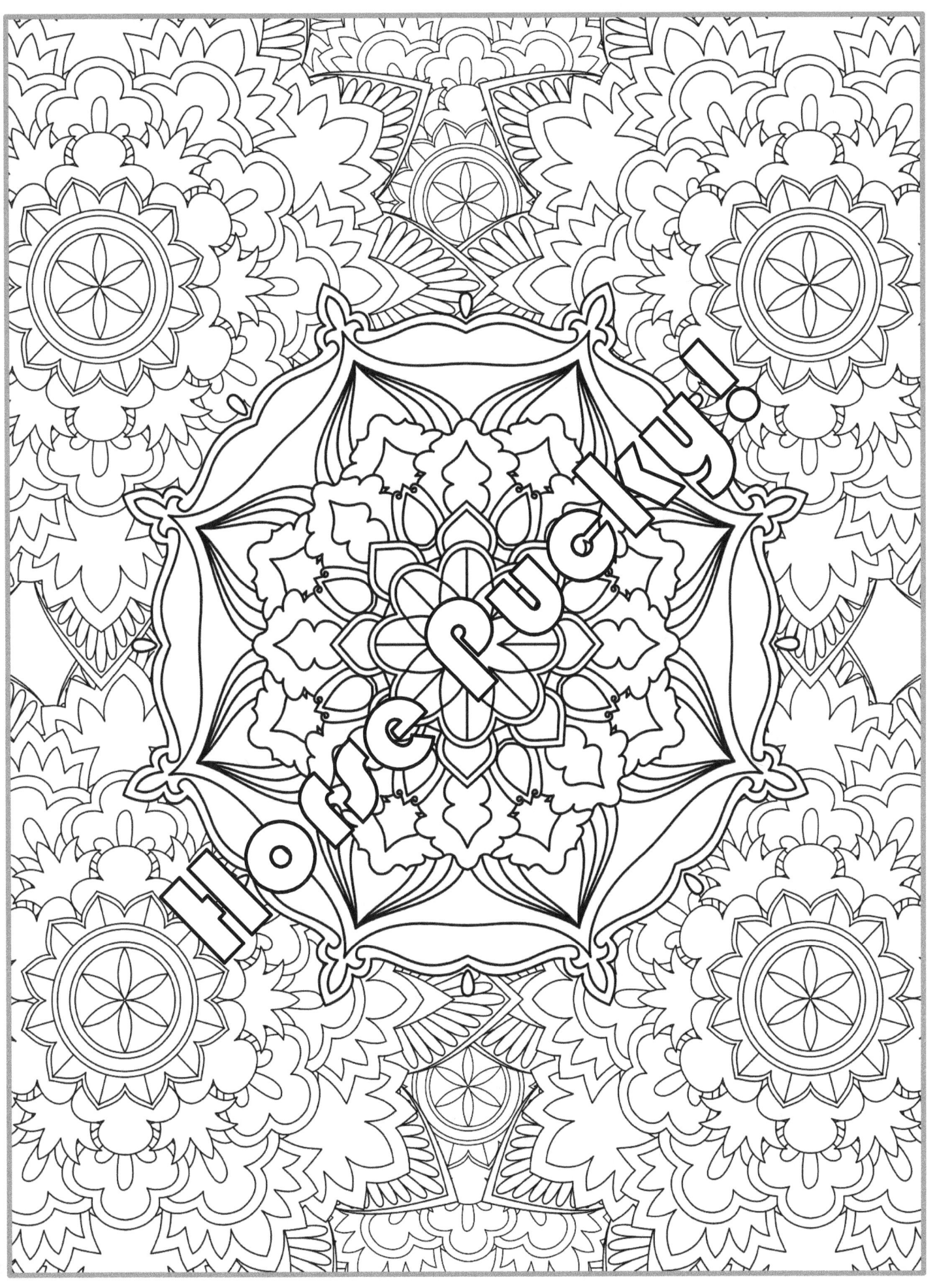

PAGE INTENTIONALLY LEFT BLANK FOR FRAMING.

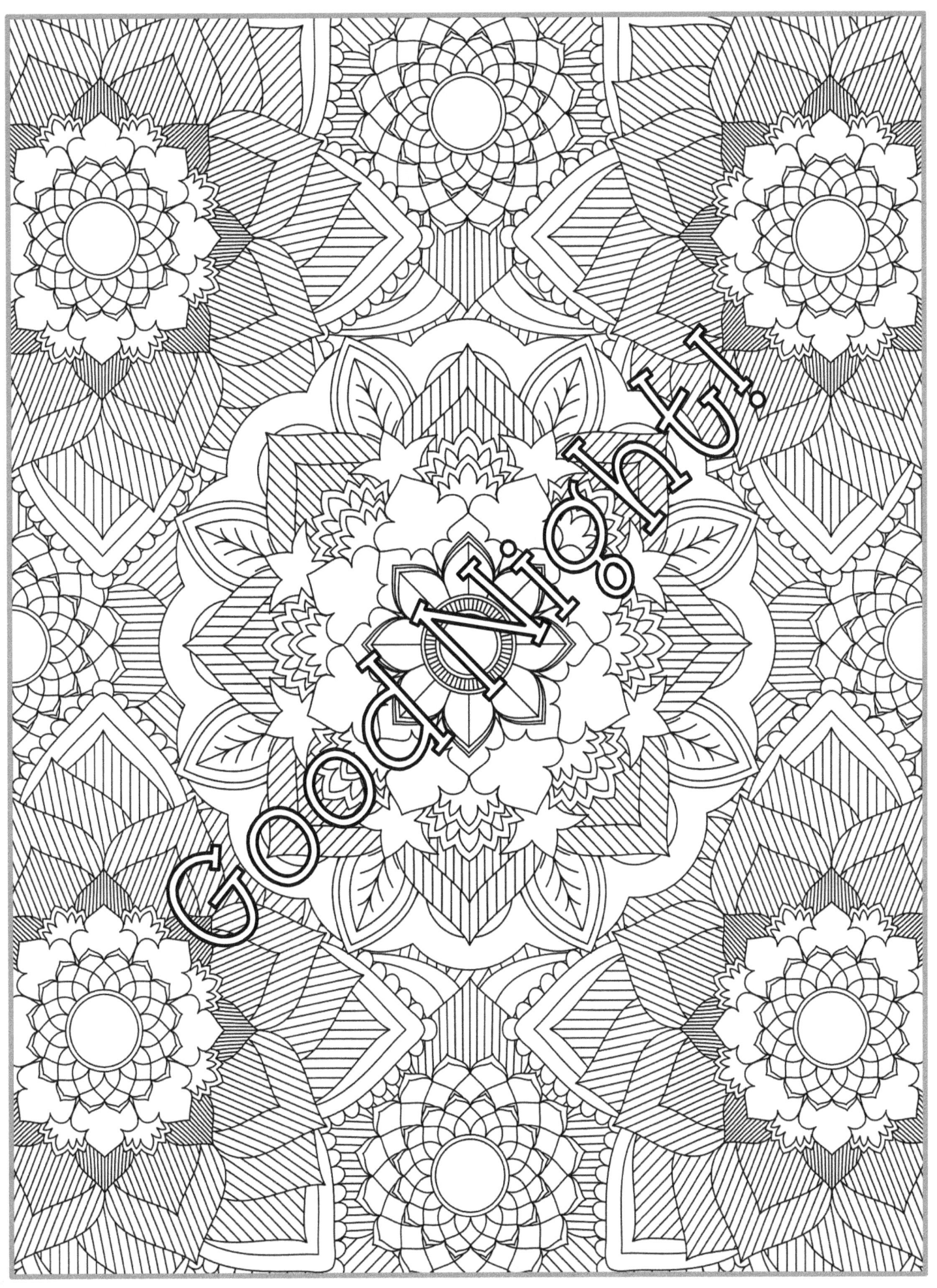

PAGE INTENTIONALLY LEFT BLANK FOR FRAMING.

PAGE INTENTIONALLY LEFT BLANK FOR FRAMING.

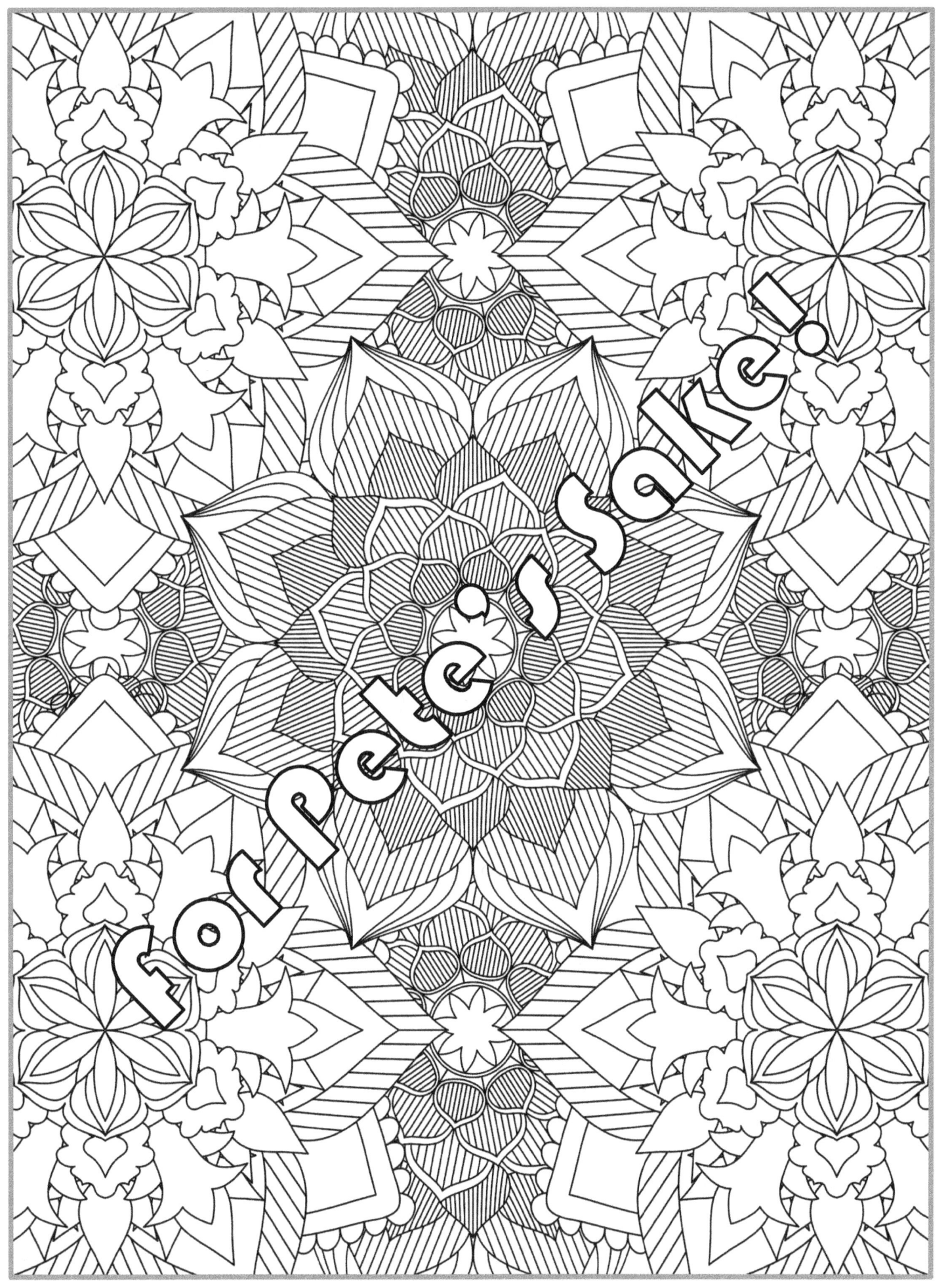

PAGE INTENTIONALLY LEFT BLANK FOR FRAMING.

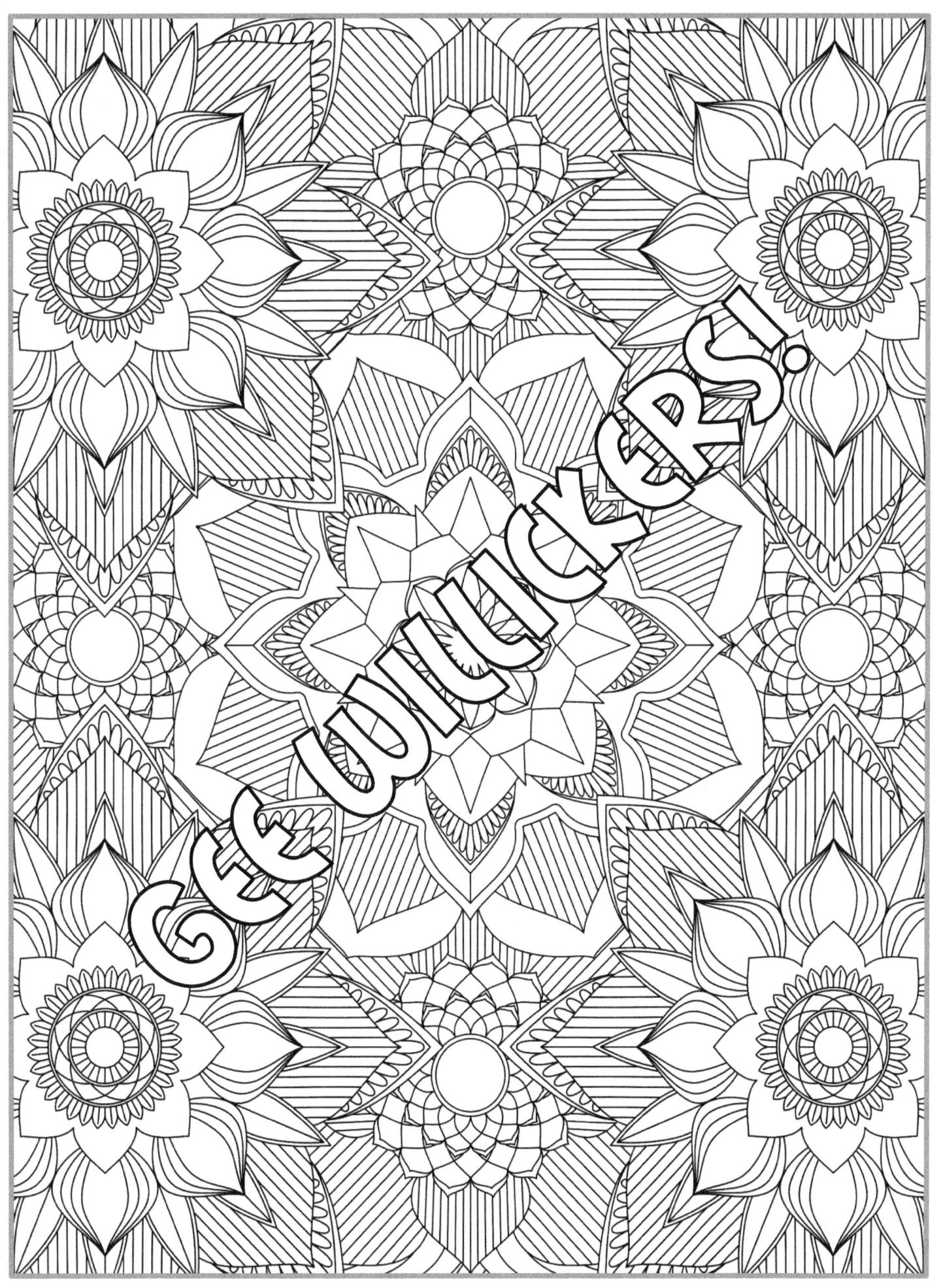

PAGE INTENTIONALLY LEFT BLANK FOR FRAMING.

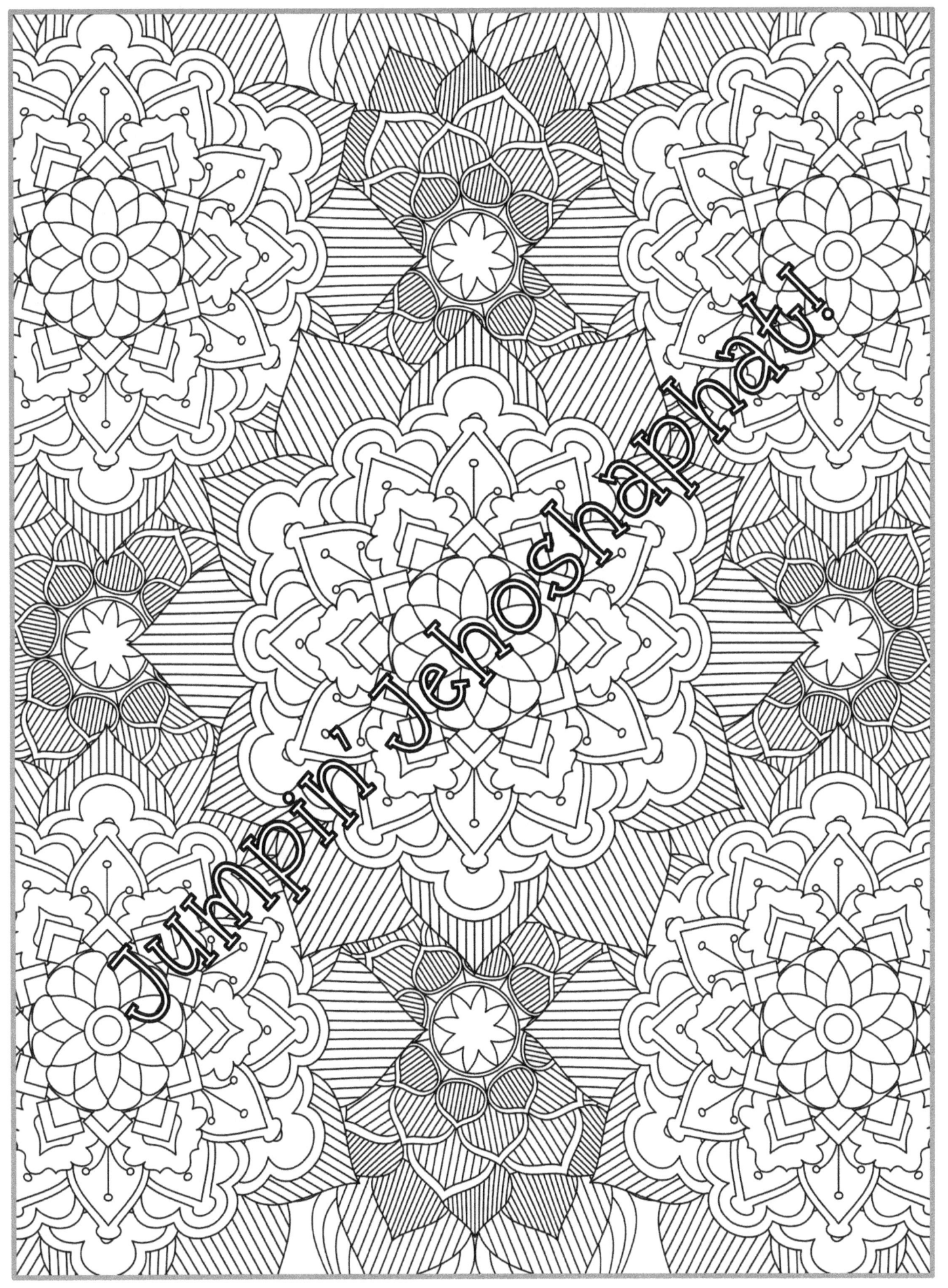

PAGE INTENTIONALLY LEFT BLANK FOR FRAMING.

PAGE INTENTIONALLY LEFT BLANK FOR FRAMING.